New Perspectives, *Past* Lives

An Exploration in Healing

Shari A. Hinkle

BALBOA
PRESS
A DIVISION OF HAY HOUSE

Copyright © 2019 Shari A. Hinkle.

All rights reserved. No part of this book may be used or reproduced by any means, graphic, electronic, or mechanical, including photocopying, recording, taping or by any information storage retrieval system without the written permission of the author except in the case of brief quotations embodied in critical articles and reviews.

Balboa Press books may be ordered through booksellers or by contacting:

Balboa Press
A Division of Hay House
1663 Liberty Drive
Bloomington, IN 47403
www.balboapress.com
1 (877) 407-4847

Because of the dynamic nature of the Internet, any web addresses or links contained in this book may have changed since publication and may no longer be valid. The views expressed in this work are solely those of the author and do not necessarily reflect the views of the publisher, and the publisher hereby disclaims any responsibility for them.

The author of this book does not dispense medical advice or prescribe the use of any technique as a form of treatment for physical, emotional, or medical problems without the advice of a physician, either directly or indirectly. The intent of the author is only to offer information of a general nature to help you in your quest for emotional and spiritual well-being. In the event you use any of the information in this book for yourself, which is your constitutional right, the author and the publisher assume no responsibility for your actions.

Any people depicted in stock imagery provided by Getty Images are models, and such images are being used for illustrative purposes only. Certain stock imagery © Getty Images.

Print information available on the last page.

ISBN: 978-1-9822-3345-7 (sc)
ISBN: 978-1-9822-3347-1 (hc)
ISBN: 978-1-9822-3346-4 (e)

Library of Congress Control Number: 2019913536

Balboa Press rev. date: 09/05/2019

To my dad, Walter Luecke, who took his final journey during my exploration. Thank you for your love and support, even from the other side.

You have no need to travel anywhere. Journey within yourself, enter a mine of rubies and bathe in the splendor of your own light.
—Rumi

Contents

Preface ix

Chapter 1   The Inexperienced Traveler 1

Chapter 2   Healings and Validations 7

Chapter 3   The Doors 11

Chapter 4   An Overdue Trip 15

Chapter 5   The Déjà Vu Spot 21

Chapter 6   Traveling through Europe 27

Chapter 7   A Journey through the Lavender Door 35

Chapter 8   A Two for One Trip 41

Chapter 9   Where There's Smoke, Is There Fire? 47

Chapter 10 The Staycation 53

Chapter 11 The Light at the End of the Tunnel 59

Chapter 12 An Unexpected Trip 65

Chapter 13 The Ultimate Journey 69

Chapter 14 Journey Back to the Islands 75

Chapter 15 The Final Piece 79

Chapter 16 Completing the Puzzle 85

Chapter 17 Coming Home 89

Acknowledgments 93

About the Author 95

Preface

Peering through a slit just wide enough for my eyes, I entered the frozen world. The multiple layers of protection made movement slow and cumbersome. Leaving those cruel Michigan winters behind me, I sought the warming comfort of the Florida sunshine. Although my body had thawed out, my true essence, my soul, had hibernated, with a sense of numbness. Perhaps there is a layering that happens over time. Could those layers be my spiritual sunscreen? But what was I keeping out? Or were the layers a barrier for keeping something in?

It has been said that we all carry around a certain amount of "baggage"—those experiences in our lives that have left their imprint. Those imprints are like random keys you find rummaging through your junk drawer, never quite remembering what lock it belongs to, but you hold on to it just in case.

Like echoes that travel through the mountains, long after the last word was spoken, so too do those imprints continue to vibrate, leaving their energetic marks deep within the body and, I believe, the soul. This provides vibrational awareness that brings us insights and information, which allows us to release blockages from physical and emotional pain so that we may heal from the past. It also, connects us to a higher source / power and gives us a greater understanding of ourselves, so that we may be freed from the layers that restrict our beliefs, growth, and compassion, bringing about fluidity of movement and thoughts.

My Background

I had worked in retail, mostly clothing, up until my early thirties. Becoming disillusioned with the corporate world and feeling like a number, I was looking for a career where I could be my own boss.

I had also become disillusioned with Western medicine. I watched my mother's health decline over the years when she was on tranquilizers. They were prescribed when her father passed away. I was *very* young. Throughout the years, as her tolerance built up, the doctors would just prescribe her stronger doses. They never questioned whether she should even be taking them; nor did they offer other options. Eventually, after I had left home, she ended up in a thirty-day rehab facility. I'm happy to report that she is drug free to this day. But the years of tranquilizers left her with physical issues that she will always be dealing with.

So, when my husband at the time suggested I look into becoming a massage therapist, I found that it filled two needs— to be my own boss and to offer alternatives to traditional medicine. Once in massage school, I realized this was my calling.

I also realized that I was sensitive to energy, the field around the physical body, and that I was drawn to this type of work. So, shortly after becoming a licensed massage therapist, I studied Therapeutic Touch with Shirley Spear Begley.

Being a licensed massage therapist and therapeutic touch practitioner for over twenty years now, I've been well aware of the "baggage" people carry around and have found some lost luggage myself. For instance, during a massage, as I began to work on a client's neck, he giggled and pulled his shoulders to his ears. He remarked, "That tickles." What was really happening was that he was going into a protection mode. Without me saying a word, he revealed to me how, as a small child, his mother would discipline him by grabbing the back of his neck. I'm sure many of you have heard someone say or even said yourself, "They're such a pain in the neck." Well, maybe they really are!

Learning and practicing as a therapeutic touch practitioner has brought me many eye- and mind-opening experiences. Therapeutic touch is an interpretation of an ancient, energy-based healing practice. It is an intentionally directed process of energy exchange that utilizes the hands to facilitate healing.

My very first workshop/course on the technique was an awakening to the power of energy and imprints left in the body. During a demonstration of the technique, a volunteer, female, sat in a chair at the front of the room. The instructor and another woman stood at each shoulder. As they began to move their hands above her physical body, from her head, over the shoulders, and downward, she burst into tears. She later revealed to the class that she had been sexually abused as a young girl by a male family member. He would approach her by placing his hand on her shoulder. And although she had been through much counseling and felt she had placed it behind her, that energetic "baggage" lay dormant in her shoulders until released. A deeper level of healing was taking place.

So, What Is This "Energy Thing"?

Energy is everything. Our thoughts, emotions and words, are all energy. So too are colors and everything in nature. And we ourselves are energetic beings. All things have their own vibration, and we are all interconnected through those vibrations. Like a stream that flows through the mountains, depending on what influences it encounters—weather, nature, humankind—energetic vibrations can look very different from beginning to end and can change from moment to moment.

Have you ever wondered why certain songs or types of music affect your moods? Why we use phrases such as "feeling blue" or "green with envy"? Maybe you've been thinking of an old friend, only to have him or her contact you out of the blue. And what about the cool chill that runs through your body when something resonates with you? What is happening is that you are interacting with those energetic vibrations.

We *all* do it. But just like a concert pianist tuning his or her piano, some people are more sensitive to those vibrations than others. I happen to be one of those people. I have always been a vivid dreamer and have even had premonitory ones at times. Certainly, my work with massage and therapeutic touch has increased my sensitivity. I can feel energetic imbalances in someone's body through my hands, without the use of physical touch. These imbalances may be there due to physical influences, such as injuries; emotional traumas; or fears. And when those imbalances are present, they can interfere with our ability to heal. Remember, we are constantly interacting with things around us. This sensitivity has been my "normal" for over twenty years.

Probably, for most people, these concepts seem foreign. You may even be wondering, *What magic carpet is she riding on?* But if you have a pioneer spirit and are willing to look beyond your comfort zone, I would love to be your tour guide on a journey of healing possibilities.

Past-Life Regression

So, what if those imprints of energy—that "baggage"—have been traveling with you, and your soul's passport shows multiple trips? Could the phobia you have, or that unexplained shoulder pain, or your desire to visit certain lands or cultures hitched a ride into this lifetime? I wondered, could *my* lack of smelling be linked to the past?

Reincarnation, or past lives, is not a new concept. Many cultures believe we have lived multiple lifetimes. And although I was raised in a Lutheran household, I have always held the belief that I have been here before. But even for me, someone who has dealt with many unusual healing techniques, past-life regression therapy was new. It held a curiosity for me, and I knew I wanted to experience it someday.

So, what exactly is this "therapy" and how does it heal? I have found that by re-experiencing a lifetime and allowing emotions (energy) from that lifetime to come forward, you are then able to release and clear them. Once that takes place, balance starts to be restored for healing.

A typical session begins with the client getting into a comfortable position. He or she is then guided into a deepened state of relaxation, also known as hypnosis, always aware of his or her present surroundings and in control *at all times*. Once the person has reached this state, he or she is then guided to a lifetime that will be beneficial for his or her healing. It is believed that the soul always knows where to go for its highest good. The hypnotist is sort of a "tour guide," helping the client unfold what is happening based on the client's feedback to questions. The client is always in the driver's seat. The hypnotist is providing the road signs. As I have found, you can experience these lifetimes in multiple ways—visually, through smell, physically, emotionally, through noise, and intuitively. Each time can be different from the last. It wasn't until I met Patricia McGivern, *my* tour guide, that I began to realize the healing my soul could experience. And I could also see that my concept of energy was about to expand to bring me multiple "awestruck" moments.

My connection to a higher power / Spirit would become stronger and more profound. Little did I know, my journeys would reunite me with my sense of smell and connect me with my father as he transitioned to the other side.

I was embarking on a journey to unpack that baggage, appreciating *all* the treasures I had carried on so many trips, finding locks that belonged to those lost keys. Who knew that, by subtracting layers, I would add pieces.

So, if that pioneer spirit resides in you and adventure is calling, let me be *your* tour guide through my journey, so that you may see the world around you and in you with different eyes than you did when you started. And if there is healing to take place, you may find it. For we are all connected, each a note vibrating through the universe, finely tuning so that the beautiful masterpiece may be heard.

Chapter 1

The Inexperienced Traveler

Curiosity was the fuel to start this journey. Faith and trust were the walking sticks to aid me when the path was unsure. Spirit was the bringer of souvenirs to validate my experiences. What I thought would be a short journey of a few sessions turned out to be a trip of a lifetime—or should I say *lifetimes*!

Patricia McGivern and I met through a mutual friend. Patti was taking part in a past-life regression project and was looking for a subject. Our friend thought I was perfect for the part. I was intrigued. Past-life regression had been on my travel itinerary for some time. So, I took a leap of faith and said yes, destination unknown.

I met Patti at her office, along with a videographer, Bobbie. Oh, did I mention I was going to be filmed? Although I felt immediately comfortable with Patti and Bobbie, the butterflies still fluttered in my stomach with unanswered questions. What would it be like? Could I even be hypnotized?

Patti and I went over any possible fears or questions I may have about the process. Since this was my first time, we decide to begin with the purpose "whatever is for my highest good."

As I settled in on her slate-blue recliner, a cozy quilt draped over me, the butterflies began to find a resting place. Surprisingly, the cameras didn't seem to bother me.

"Close your eyes and take some nice deep breaths," Patti's calming voice began.

Little did I know this would be the start of a journey that would change *this* lifetime by visiting many of my soul's previous lifetimes.

Patti continued with some guided relaxation techniques. Some of this was familiar, as I'd used similar techniques myself during massage. The butterflies were still. I could feel any resistance leaving my muscles. The chair and I became one.

"Now, imagine a set of ancient stairs in front of you. As you walk down them, they lead you to a beautiful garden." Patti's voice was my focus. By this point I was blissfully relaxed. Time was irrelevant.

Now, this is very important. At no point was I asleep. Nor did I forget where my fifty-year-old body was parked.

Patti guided me to a long hallway with many doors. "Look and see if a door speaks to you," she suggested. I saw only one door in the hallway. Patti encouraged me to open it. I pushed open the rustic wooden door before me and found myself entering another lifetime!

Whoa! Looking out, I saw nothing but rolling green hills, with no trees or bushes in sight. I recognized it as the Great Plains. I relayed this to Patti, and she had me look down at my hands and feet.

"Can you tell me how old you are?" she inquired.

There they were! The dirty, bare feet of a seven-year-old girl. I could see them! I also saw the sleeves of the thin cotton dress I was wearing. The sun caught the streaks of my loosely braided, light brown hair. It was as if I was watching a movie, and I was in the lead role.

Patti sat next to me and took notes as I relayed what I saw.

Something in the distance caught my eye. A rugged man with salt-and-pepper hair rode up on his horse. I believed him to be my father in that life.

"Look into his eyes; does your soul recognize a connection?" said Patti's voice.

I found nothing familiar.

"I'd like you to go to the place where you live," suggested Patti.

The house was a small wooden structure with a narrow front porch. Someone was standing there, a slender woman wearing an apron that covered a long cotton dress. Her brown hair was pulled back in a bun, revealing her tanned face. I believed she was my mother from that life.

Once again, Patti had me look into her eyes. "Does your soul recognize a connection?"

An emotion bubbled up. I really didn't want to cry on camera, but the tears came anyway. As sure as she was my mother then, she was also my mother presently! Now, there was a turn in the road I hadn't seen coming.

It was right around this time of soul recognition that something grabbed my attention. Now, remember that energy thing I mentioned earlier? I experienced a rush of coolness flowing down the front of me, starting at my shoulders. Like the mist that releases from the freezer on a hot day, it blanketed me. With my knowledge and sensitivity to energy, I was aware that an energetic release had just taken place. I quickly learned it was related to the kidney meridian, or energy pathway, as my bladder began to speak to me. But was this sensation real? I set it aside; I wasn't about to stop now!

Ignoring my bladder, I pushed onward. Patti said, "When I snap my fingers, you'll tell me your name. One, two, three." *Snap.*

Effortlessly, the name Laura flowed out of my mouth. "Laura Smith."

Patti then had me move time forward. "What do you see?"

I was on a wooden platform beside a train. Now in my twenties, I was smartly dressed in a long tailored dress with matching hat. My now brown hair was neatly pulled off my face. My clothing suggested the year was in the 1800s. I believed the city was San Francisco.

I made my way to a yellow two-story structure labeled "Mrs. Murdock's Boarding School." This was where I live. I relayed this to Patti. Upon entering the structure, I saw several young women dressed similarly to me, sitting around.

Patti instructed me to move time forward again. "Where do you work?"

I was in a retail store where cloth was sold for dressmaking. Now, mind you, the awareness of my bladder was starting to speak louder. It was most definitely a real urge. But I didn't want to stop.

"What is the next significant thing you remember?"

There was an earthquake happening. Mild shaking of the building was taking place.

"When I snap my fingers, you'll tell me what year it is." Patti snapped her fingers.

Okay, now, this is where you may want to buckle your seatbelts. We're about to hit some turbulence. In answer to Patti's question, the year 1-9-8-7 moved past my lips. Each number came with hesitation, but I was unable to stop it. My conscious brain was trying its hardest not to let those numbers come out. It was reminding me that I was born in 1963! But that wasn't all. Now I was no longer Laura, but Mark Faulkner, a gay white male in his twenties. I could see my contorted body lying in the street. There were fires and chaos around me. From the contusion on my forehead, I realized I had suffered a head trauma that I wouldn't survive. The connection was the city, and in Mark's life, a major earthquake was taking place. What the heck had just happened?

I sensed Patti was a little surprised too. And as if this wasn't enough, now my bladder was overruling my mind, and I whispered to Patti that I needed to use the restroom. As I said in the beginning, you are always aware of your surroundings. But would I be able to get back into this space of Mark? I could only hope.

I used the restroom, and then, thanks to Patti's expertise, I was able to slip right back into the blissful state.

Before we explored Mark's life, Patti brought me back to the lifetime of Laura. "I want you to go back to the last day of your life as Laura." Patti's voice was once again my focus.

I was lying on a bed; my hands suggested that I had made it into my senior years. There was a younger woman at my bedside. I knew I had never married or had children, so I wasn't sure who she was. I felt very happy and peaceful in my passing.

Patti then had me return to my life as Mark. There was sadness and regret for leaving my lover too soon.

Patti brought me out of the regression. There were still some residual emotions lingering regarding Mark's lifetime and passing.

A multitude of thoughts and emotions were running through my head, including exhilaration, exhaustion, and confusion. I was struggling with the concept of my soul being in two places at once. Was that possible? I had never been to San Francisco in my current life. And although I was instructed not to do any research, Patti discovered that, in fact, a major earthquake took place in 1987!

Chapter 2

Healings and Validations

The train had left the station, destination unknown, taking me to a foreign land with more questions than answers. Had those lives really happened? Or had I made it all up with information already in my mind? Was it possible for a soul to be in two bodies at the same time? I prayed for guidance and confirmation to make sense of it all. I wanted that artifact—that proof to satisfy my questioning mind.

By the time I arrived home that Saturday from Patti's, my body was so exhausted that getting off the couch was an effort. It was as if my mind were an energetic pot that had been stirred; information was flooding my awareness. But when I would close my eyes and try to rest, visions of faces and names appeared in my mind, making sleep a challenge. My journey had officially begun, and the best was yet to come.

Three days after the regression, it was already on my agenda to get labs done for my kidney doctor and see my acupuncturist. For the past nine years, I had seen my acupuncturist on a quarterly basis. These visits were to keep everything balanced and to help me stay well. I had not told him about the regression, and I was curious what he would find regarding my kidney meridian. That day he found it to be a little weak. When I informed him of my experiences with Patti, he found it interesting that it had affected one of my strongest meridians. His assessment validated that the cool chill I had felt early in the regression was, in fact, my kidney meridian. The true healing would come a week later.

Even after seeing my acupuncturist, I was still struggling with questions. Had I fabricated everything in my mind? Could my soul really be in two bodies at the same time? Did I have enough faith and trust in something greater to just accept what I intuitively knew at a soul level? Those thoughts resonated through the universe like a call button on an airplane. Once that call was sent out, Spirit responded.

The Saturday after seeing Patti, as I waited for my first client, I grabbed a magazine to pass the time. *Bam*! I opened it up to a view I had seen a week ago in my regression. It was the Great Plains, just as I had seen it (minus a buffalo). After picking my jaw up off the floor, I grabbed another magazine. *Bam*! There I found an article on the City of San Francisco. Now I'd seen both locations from my regression. Okay, Spirit, you definitely have my attention.

A week after seeing my acupuncturist, I was in the exam room of my kidney doctor awaiting the results of my lab work.

A few years back, I had been diagnosed with a kidney condition. My left kidney had a weak filter. My mother had an advanced version, on the same side, which she was now on medication for. I was seeing my doctor yearly to monitor the condition. After looking over the lab work, he said everything was now normal, and I no longer needed to see him. My mind was blown! That was firsthand validation of my belief that, by releasing, shifting, and balancing our energy, we could heal our physical bodies. Now after several years, the condition still has not returned.

Between the healing and validations, maybe I *could* let go and trust the guidance of something greater than myself. After all, isn't that the point of a foreign land—to explore!

My mind was still very active from the session with Patti; a red exterior door began appearing in my mind's eye. What was this all about? I would soon find out.

Chapter 3

The Doors

Awareness is a funny thing. Traveling familiar, routine routes somewhat dulls the mind. We tend to go on a sort of "autopilot." We stop *seeing* until awareness reawakens us. And so it was with the red door.

My guy and I fish for bass. One place we have fished *many* times is the Hillsborough River. We have cruised up and down the same stretch of river looking for "the bite." This day was no different than any other day, until awareness hit me in the face with a big red door on the front of a house. The very next thing I was drawn to were the house numbers, 1102. Could this be a message from Spirit? And if so, what?

A few days later, on our house-hunting quest, we went to look at a house. As we pulled up, I couldn't help but notice the red door and the house number, 11502. Now I was really intrigued.

They say the third time's a charm. And I have found for me, personally, Spirit tends to bring me validations in threes. On the way home from that appointment, awareness snuck in on a route that we'd traveled hundreds of times. A mailbox stood out with the numbers 1102! Okay, I got it. I was listening. But what did 1102 mean?

I have utilized *Sacred Scribe Angel Numbers* many times in the past to gain clarity when certain numbers keep showing up. So, that was exactly where I turned. The master number 11 speaks about a spiritual awakening and connecting with our soul's mission. It also speaks about developing your spiritual aspects and serving your divine life purpose. The number *2* resonates with energies of faith and trust. And *0* is considered to represent the beginning of a spiritual journey. Well, that gave me a lot to think about and contemplate. I believe that "cool mist" felt during the regression was just that, a shift, an awakening, and a thinning of the "veil" to connect with Spirit more clearly. This trip, this journey I had started, had opened a new land before me that I was bursting to explore! Now the red door wasn't the only one showing up in my mind.

The second door to meander in was a lavender one. This time it appeared whimsical, "hobbit-like." It didn't take long for it to show up, either. During an evening walk with my man and our dog, in our quaint little town, there it was! My lavender door had a whimsical window at the top. It was the front door to a shop known as Indigo Fire and Dragon Shoppe. Okay, Spirit, please clarify.

Boy, I tell you, Spirit is quick. As we continued on our walk, we passed another store with two big display windows. The windows were full of various pieces of wooden signs with things printed on them. Front and center, a piece caught my eye. Printed on it was the word *dragon*. Okay, now at least I had a direction to go. A few days later, as I was looking through images of starry nights on the computer, right there in the middle of all those nighttime pictures—can you guess?—yes, a picture of a dragon popped up! That was number three.

But I wondered, friend or foe?

So, once again, I turned to the internet to search dragon pictures to see if any spoke to me. One grabbed my heart; it featured a girl sitting across from her dragon, in silhouette, reading a book. I felt, as odd as this may sound, a kinship with them. Most definitely, it was friend! But why did Spirit show me this? That answer awaited me in another regression.

I was learning that Spirit tended to bring me things in threes. The doors were no different. The third door I saw was a bright yellow exterior door. This one had a feeling of "career" attached to it. There was also a sense that this was going to be down the road.

About a month after seeing Patti for the regression, I was leaving my doctor's office—again traversing a route I had traveled multiple times. There was awareness showing up, a bright yellow door on a home. My eye was instantly drawn to the street sign, which read "Skycrest." Okay, that meant nothing to me.

So, I decided to google it and see what came up. The very first thing to show up was "Skycrest Schools." Was this for me? Was I to become a teacher of some sort? Or maybe, a student. I wouldn't know the answer for almost a year.

Chapter 4

An Overdue Trip

Hopefully, you've never had the experience of sitting on a plane, excited to be jetting off on an adventure, when someone comes over the speaker and announces, "We need to have everyone come off the plane due to issues beyond our control." So, it happened after my first regression. The plan was to film three to four regressions, but Spirit put a fork in the road. The project kept getting delayed time after time, and eventually my "trip" was canceled after approximately six months from the first regression. So, there I was, excited and then very disappointed. I knew I *had* to explore more with Patti, even if it was on my own. But when that should be was unclear. So, I waited in limbo.

Although a year had passed since that incredible experience, the details were still fresh in my mind. As I sat at an intersection that I traveled through daily, there was awareness in the form of a billboard for Skycrest Schools! It was my yellow door, Skycrest; Spirit was calling me. It was time for the student to go back to school, and Patti was to be my teacher. This time there were no cameras—just Patti and me, the recliner, and the quilt—and the butterflies returning with questions. Could I be hypnotized again? Would I see things as clearly as I had the first time?

The concern was wasted, as I slipped into hypnosis quite easily.

"You'll be in a hallway with many doors," Patti guided.

Minor panic set in. Nope, no hallway, no doors, just darkness. Patti suggested I feel for the doors. Nope, still dark. It wasn't until she suggested I feel my feet on the floor and clothes against my skin that it dawned on me. Oh, I'm *already* in a lifetime.

I realized I was barefoot, on a dirt floor. It was a cellar, a dark cellar. I had an awareness of light cotton clothing hanging from my slender, twenty-something male body. *Whoa, I'm a black slave.*

"I'd like you to rewind the scene, like a video, before that incident. What do you see?" she inquired.

I was a young boy either in Mississippi or Louisiana. Many siblings surrounded me, but I was particularly close to an older sister. As I looked into her eyes, there was something familiar but no definite recognition.

"When I snap my fingers, you'll tell me your name. Three, two, one." Patti snapped her fingers.

Without hesitation, "Samuel, Samuel Jackson," left my mouth. I was aware it was sometime in the 1800s.

"What's the next significant event you remember?" inquired Patti.

Men had come in the middle of the night. They were taking my siblings and me to be sold as slaves. I was so happy, and now I felt scared and closed off. I would never see my family again.

As Patti instructed me to move time forward, a beautiful home came into view. Full-grown oak trees lined the long drive, leading up to a stunning two-story home. There were full porches on both levels, and columns rose from ground to roof. I knew this was a Southern plantation home. I also was aware that this plantation dealt more with raising food than with cotton. I was realizing that this regression was going quite differently than the first one had. It has more "still scenes" and was less movie-like. Maybe it was due to the fact that, as Samuel, I felt isolated and withdrawn. I didn't know; this was still so new to me.

I didn't get a sense of too many people around me. Again, maybe it was that closed-off feeling.

"What do you do?" Patti probed.

I worked in the stables—not as a "stable boy." I was in charge of the horses. I found myself particularly fond of an old gray mare.

Once again, Patti had me move time forward. There was a fire in the main house. It burned to the ground, but I sensed no one was hurt. But now where had I gone? I realized I had accompanied the master to Clarkston, Louisiana. I was still in charge of the horses.

Aha! I knew why I was in the cellar now. My *employer*, no longer my master, had passed away. I was being relieved of my duties, much to my dismay. I put up quite a fuss, and had been put by someone, though I wasn't sure who, in the cellar to cool down.

Patti instructed me to move time forward. I could see myself walking down a dirt road, still in the South, where my wife waited for me at home.

Patti then instructed me to go to the last day of my life. I hadn't grown too awfully old. I was in bed, with my wife sitting beside me. I passed from a respiratory ailment.

A frequently asked question after passing was, "What were you supposed to learn in that lifetime?" As Samuel, I believe it was to balance work and play.

Then, Patti had me go to a higher place, where a wise and loving being came to me. Before me, I saw this brilliant white light; no figure was visible. It conveys that, *you are loved, and you are lovable.* Overwhelmed with emotion, I felt the tears begin to fall.

Once I was emerged from the regression, I realized that I was nowhere near as tired as I had been the first time. This one also had less detail and more "sensing." Still, the logical mind was trying to undermine the experience. But, deep down, I knew different. This was no mirage. But just to satisfy that skeptic side of my brain, I put it out there anyway. "Spirit, please bring me validation." Boy, let me tell you, Spirit is quick, and what a jaw-dropping validation it was!

Spirit wasted no time. Two days after my session, I was training a Pilates client. She, too, was an entrepreneur, so when her phone went off indicating she received a text, she assumed it was her assistant. I was totally caught off guard by what happened next. Now, mind you, she had no knowledge of the past-life regression work I was doing. She responded to hearing her phone, "That would be the plantation manager. She's such a slave driver!"

It was all I could do not to react to what I had just heard. I didn't reveal anything to her then. We finished her session like normal.

With her departure, I was left with gratitude for Spirit's quick and powerful response. But I was also left with more questions. Could my regression have shifted the energy of Samuel closer to the surface, allowing her to pick up on it subconsciously? Had the two of us been connected in a past life?

That wouldn't be the last time she'd leave me awestruck.

Chapter 5

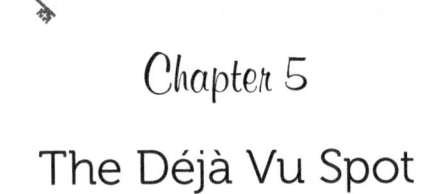

The Déjà Vu Spot

I was on a journey with no exact destination or time frame in mind. This trip was a year in the making, and I had an open-ended ticket.

A month after my life as Samuel, I arrived in Patti's office. A few butterflies still fluttered about, but they quickly found a place to rest. I went into hypnosis quite easily now. But before Patti could get to the part of the "hallways and doors," my attention was being drawn to a familiar place—a place where Spirit and I had connected many times in my mind. It was a place of rebalancing and rejuvenation when life got challenging. For you, it may be a beach scene or in the mountains or maybe a beautiful garden. For me, there is a column that rises from the canyon floor in the Southwest. As I sat atop this column, the approaching sunset lent itself to warmth without the heat. The gentle wind on my face and through my hair felt like Mother Earth's caress. My connection to the Great Spirit was powerful in this place. But why had remained a mystery, until now.

As my relaxation deepened, so too did my awareness of this place. My long black hair of a younger native woman gently moved with the breath of the wind, while the sun warmed my face, looking out onto the canyon of red rocks. Lying in the recliner, I felt the tears begin to flow. A puzzle piece of realization fit into place—a realization that the comfort and calm I had felt atop my column was because I'd been here before! My soul knew and was holding that energy of connectedness to this land for me.

When Patti asked, I was unaware of the year or the tribe. But I believe we were nomadic, as we had no village at the time. "We sleep under the stars." A smile grew on my face as I relayed this to Patti. Even today, star gazing brings peace and calm to me. Our group was small in numbers. As I surveyed the location around me, I saw a gentle river meandering through the red rock. Then Patti asked me my name. I heard the word *Hiawatha*. But I knew this was not quite accurate.

"Move time forward," Patti suggested.

We were under attack at our camp by the river. My focus was on protecting the children. Patti inquired if I knew who was attacking us. It is another tribe, possibly Apache. It saddened me that they would want to hurt us. We were a peaceful people.

Patti had me move time forward. We were many now, and I was an old woman. It felt as if we were farther north—Flagstaff, Arizona, I thought. There was a "wall" of pine trees behind me.

"Do you hold a place in the tribe?" Patti wondered.

I knew I was an elder who was held in high honor.

Next, she asked, "Are you married?"

There was no definite sense of a husband, but I used pronouns like "we" and "us," so I thought so.

"Any children?" Patti continued.

Immediately, I responded, "They are all our children." *Where did that come from?* I thought.

"I'd like you to go to the last day of your life," said Patti's voice.

There was a lone tree that I was lying under. Something struck me as odd. My clothing was very vibrant, with reds, yellows, and blues. It felt out of place. A sense of urgency began to rise as Patti was taking me through the death scene. My mind is telling me, *Come on already. I want to go home.* It felt as if this "Earth walk" was just a visit. It all felt different somehow.

A wise and loving being generally came forward once you ascended. This time was different from the last. Standing before me was a tall, slender man. His white hair peaked out of his hooded taupe robe. He took hold of my hands. Words were unnecessary as a profound sense of peace filled my being.

"What was it that you were supposed to learn in this lifetime?" Patti wondered.

Connecting with Spirit—that was my lesson.

She then helped me emerge from the regression.

With not much information to go on, I was unsure as to how I would be able to research anything. But my soul was providing me with clues. For days following the regression, I kept hearing a "ch" sound in my head relating to the tribe. The tribes I was familiar with—Cheyenne, Chippewa, and Cherokee—didn't feel right. So, the trusty internet was where I turned to research, typing in "Southwestern tribes." A word caught my eye, *kachina*, which seemed to be calling to me to investigate. I soon became educated on the Hopi Tribe of the Southwest. In their belief system were spirit beings who, many moons ago, were to have walked with the humans on the Earth. These beings were known as kachinas. It was believed they were the link between gods and mortals. In the Hopi religion, the kachina were said to reside in the San Francisco Peaks near Flagstaff, Arizona!

So, being the visual person that I am, I searched images of the San Francisco Peaks. My mouth dropped open as I stare at a line, one might even say a "wall," of pine trees—just like in my regression. Now wait; that wasn't all. My research also revealed that the kachinas wore brightly colored clothing! The dots were starting to connect.

The Hopis had a vast amount of kachinas in their religion. Some were for rain, others were for crops, and on and on. I noticed the *wuya* were considered the most important. So, I decided to scroll down their names. Could there be one close to Hiawatha? I wondered. There it was, "Hahay-i-wuhti." She was known as the mother of all kachinas and was married to Eototo, the chief of all kachinas. Goose bumps ran up and down my body. That explained my brightly colored clothing in the death scene and the feeling of "going home."

But was I trying to force the pieces of the puzzle to fit? Spirit would soon provide me with the answer.

Having been to the Southwest and Sedona, specifically, I was very aware of Kokopelli, the flute player. What I was not aware of was the fact that he was a kachina. Still seeking validation, I was happy to find that Spirit wasted no time. Within a few days after seeing Patti, as I waited in a drive-through lane, staring back at me from the window of the car in front of me was Kokopelli! This was quite common to see out West, but not so much so in Florida. Not only was I learning new things by researching the sessions, but I was also being shown how Spirit speaks to us when we are present and listening. I was looking forward to my next session with Patti. Who knew where I would be exploring next?

Chapter 6

Traveling through Europe

Just like traveling, where there are constants—baggage check, security, boarding—so too are there constants with the regressions. Similar verbiage was used each time to induce that deeply relaxed hypnotic state. But the journeys, as well as the destinations, could be quite different each time, as I was finding out.

Unlike the last two, my August session was very detailed. As Patti was nearing the hallways and doors part, I began to see myself in a beautiful dress of the 1600s—the style where your bosoms are pushed up and "on display." I was already in the lifetime. The sunlight streamed through the windows that ran the full length of the hallway I found myself in, matching my mood of happy and carefree. My stylish, well-kept blond hair and fancy dress lent me to believe I was of privilege. Patti suggested I go to a window and look outside. "What do you see?" A beautiful manicured lawn was only interrupted by a gravel horseshoe drive running through it. There were really no trees or bushes around. It felt like France or England.

Having a few regressions behind me now, I was very comfortable relaying information to Patti, especially the answers to the "typical" questions. "Antoinette" rolled off my tongue when I was asked my name. I lived in this chateau with my Aunt Helene and Uncle Bernard. I got a sense that they had raised me.

Patti instructed me to move time forward. It was now nighttime, and I was seated next to a handsome young man at a long wooden table. There was some sort of party or gathering my aunt and uncle were throwing in a large banquet hall. The mood was very uplifted and flirtatious.

But soon after this scene, I observed my uncle outside of the chateau engaged in conversation with people from the town. The feeling quickly took on a more serious nature. Something was wrong. We had to flee that night for our safety.

We traveled by carriage. Maneuvering on narrow roads lined with tall, slender trees was no easy task by night. As we came to an opening, a magnificent castle rose up, extending a stone bridge to cross over a moat. Even at night, the spires that reached upward were very vivid. I believed our journey had taken us to Germany. There was darkness that resided with this place. My uncle and the lord of the castle are connected somehow. That was why we'd come here; we'd be safe. The lord, a tall dark-haired man, left me feeling uncomfortable. I was aware of his gaze that held unwanted advances.

As Patti had me move time forward, I found myself in what appeared to be the castle's chapel. I was dressed in this magnificent ice blue satin ... wedding dress! Although, I was quite unhappy at this thought, I realized my impending marriage was expected and that I was doing it "out of duty" on my part. I couldn't help but notice how much information and detail I was getting in this regression. Also, an awareness was present of the extreme shift from light, bright, and happy to a dark, oppressed feeling. It was that darkness that continued.

As Patti had me move time forward once again, I was now dressed in a white cotton nightshirt of sorts. My body was sweating, and I was pulling my thighs to my chest. *Oh my gosh, I'm giving birth!* I brought into this world a beautiful baby girl. Sara was her name, I believe. And in that instance of giving birth, light and joy flooded my awareness. It was as if no one else existed but her and me. It was almost overwhelming, this joy I felt.

As time progressed, Sara was now a young girl, and we were in a beautiful sunlit garden. It felt like we were back at the chateau. It didn't matter where we were, for I was with her. She was my life.

"I would like you to go to the last day of your life," said Patti's voice.

I find myself in a large four-poster canopy bed. Sara, now a young lady, was sitting beside me. Oddly, I felt no sadness. There was this *knowing* that we would share other lives together. The transition was peaceful.

"What were you supposed to learn as Antoinette?" This

was one of Patti's regular questions. The answer came without hesitation and was crystal clear. "Without the dark, you can't have the light." Also, the lesson was to be grateful for *All* of it.

My "wise and loving being" stepped forward. It was my aunt and uncle from that life. They wanted to be sure I understood why things had to happen the way they did. And I understood.

Patti had something new for me this time. "Imagine you are in an ancient library. What do you see?"

It was very old, with lots of wood and books from floor to ceiling.

Patti continued, "Is there a book that speaks to you?"

I was drawn to a red one, high up on a shelf.

"Take it down. Is there a title?" Patti inquires.

Gratitude was spelled out in bold gold letters.

"Open it. What does it say?" Patti wondered.

There were no words, just a large red heart filling the page. I felt the need to hold it to my chest, "heart to heart."

As I came out of hypnosis, I brought with me this immense sense of gratitude. There was so much detail and emotion in this regression. It was much different than the last two. And boy, did it stir up some energy!

Sleep was restless that night. This internal heat kept waking me. And yes, even though I was of a certain age, it was not hormones creating it. Rather, the heat I felt was similar to the heat I'd experienced while giving a massage during which the energy was shifting. *My* energy was shifting, awakening.

It was still present upon rising, but so too was the profound sense of gratitude—so much so that tears filled my eyes on the way to work. It was if I was overflowing with it. But even before I left for work, Spirit was present and brought validation. A commercial on the TV showed a woman opening a piece of paper, with only a big red heart on it. But that was just the tip of the iceberg for what would show up later that day.

My first client of the day was a repeat massage client. About midway through her massage, that internal heat finally began to subside—only to be replaced, rather quickly, by a cramping sensation in my lower pelvic region. Simultaneously, my low back began to ache. The first image to flash into my mind was labor pains—Antoinette giving birth! Just to clarify, I had given birth in this lifetime but no longer possessed a uterus. I continue the massage, saying nothing to my client. The sensation didn't leave me. Okay, ten minutes went by and nothing was changing. So, mentally I asked, *Mine or someone else's?*

In that instant, the sensation disappeared, followed by a warm rush of energy. Questions raced through my mind. Was it possible, that I had carried that energy forward from that lifetime and was reexperiencing it? And if so, was I able to release and balance it for potential healing? Or maybe, my client was having cramps, and I had just picked up on it. Spirit would soon clarify it for me.

Within an hour of that massage client leaving, I had started training three Pilates clients on the reformers (equipment designed specifically for Pilates). It had been raining, so I left the room to retrieve a towel for one of them. I returned just in time to hear one of them say, "like childbirth." But wait, that wasn't all. It was the same client who'd made the "plantation" remarks from the earlier regression as Samuel. Hard as it was, I remained silent. All of it left my head spinning. Spirit was listening and had *delivered* the answer!

Being very visual, I wanted to see if I could identify the castle in Germany. Searching through images via the internet, I indeed came upon it; as soon as I saw it, I knew it was Eltz Burg Castle. The spires, the moat, the trees leading up to the castle—they were all there. I had to tell Patti.

But it wasn't until a week later that, once again, Spirit would blow my mind with a validation. As I waited for take-out, I decided to search through more images of Eltz Burg Castle. Oh my goodness, I couldn't believe what I was looking at—a woman on the bridge, who, from the back, could've been me, holding a red, heart-shaped Mylar balloon! I couldn't help but recall the book in the ancient library, *Gratitude*, the red heart on the page. Wait until I show this to Patti!

I'd started this journey out of curiosity about past-life regression. But a shift was starting to take place in me. Trust and connection to Spirit was growing. My strong sense of intuition was becoming even stronger. I was beginning to find a richer sense of self-acceptance and assurance—coming to welcome the sensitivities to energy and intuition that, in childhood, I'd found could can often be viewed as challenging character traits. But most of all, my view of energy and healing were expanding, and I started to see our souls, energy in a whole new way.

Questions began filling my mind: Does the soul become multilayered over lifetimes? If the energy from traumas, be they physical or emotional, isn't cleared or balanced from each lifetime, does it create layers? And if we carry those layers forward, can we create physical illness in our present lives?

I had no doubt the cramping I'd experienced during that massage was an energetic imprint, brought closer to the surface from the regression work.

But I was also beginning to realize that, as energies were shifting and layers were being pulled back, I was starting to sense and "see" more into the past. One such incident happened while I was giving a massage. It was my last client of what had been a long Saturday. The music of choice, Celtic, was playing. I'd always been drawn to that music. It touches my heart deeply. I began sensing and then seeing in my mind myself as a young woman. It was either Ireland or Scotland; I wasn't sure. Then the name *Mohra* came to mind.

Now remember those adventuresome minds I asked you to bring along on this journey? I sensed it was a lifetime of Merlin, magic, dragons, and fairies. I know, I know. Remember, open minds. All destinations are possible. Could this be the life connected to the lavender door and dragons? It amazed me how Spirit responds to our questions. The very next day, as I was watching the news, a story came on about a man. No, he didn't have a dragon, but his last name was *Mora*!

I decided it was time to put a destination on this journey that I had begun back in April 2016. The itinerary turned into a treasure map of sorts, and "X marks the spot" was my sense of smell. As far as I knew, I could never remember having one, or losing it. Who knew if I would indeed find it? But I knew one thing for sure. I was up for the adventure. And let me tell you, what an adventure it was!

Chapter 7

A Journey through the Lavender Door

Stepping into a world that was only read about in fairytales takes a traveler who is open to *all* possibilities. A sense of adventure and curiosity is a must. I had nothing to lose. But boy, what I was about to gain!

October's session had a road map that the previous sessions had not. While we always trusted that the soul goes where it needs to for our highest good, this time we also added direction. We were looking for the lifetime that related to my lack of smelling in this lifetime. At the beginning of the relaxation part, Patti had me envision a light entering at the crown of my head. Very quickly, I become aware of a *pulsing* in between my eyebrows. This area is also known as the third-eye chakra or energy center.

This is where intuition is said to reside. This was totally new to me—never, in or out of our sessions, had I experienced anything like this. *Cool*, I thought. But that wasn't the only new thing that was about to happen. The previous regressions I'd had either entered lifetimes after I went through a door or I just started sensing/seeing images. This time, my nose led the way. I started smelling smoke!

There I stood, a sixteen year-old-girl, hair of fire red, and pale white skin smudged with dirt. I recognized that I was in that lifetime I had recently previewed. I was Mohra. Terror ran through me as I witnessed my entire village of stone huts with thatched roofs ablaze. Scotland was the country, I believed. People were running and screaming in chaos.

"What do you do?" Patti inquired.

Tears began to stream down my face as I uttered the words, "I don't know what to do."

Patti detected a sense of panic in my voice and reassured me it was okay. "Do you know who did this?" Patti asked.

There were horses, men dressed in metal linked armor. I believe they were the English. Guilt started to overwhelm me, for everyone perished. I would've been there, had it not been for one thing. I was in the hills with my dragon. Yes, I said dragon!

Patti had me move time forward. My home was now a castle. I was in a room with bottles and potions, a laboratory of sorts. I noticed a cot, my bed, off to the side. Merlin had taken me under his care to teach me the ways of nature, healing, and magic. I was also known as a "seer"—like a psychic would be today. The location of the castle was unknown to me, but I believed the king's name to be Edward. Patti suggests to "move time forward" again.

Merlin advised me it was time for him to leave this dimension, and I was ready to take over. Time moved on, and I found myself surrounded by beautiful purple flowers. Their tiny, little faces, illuminated by the sun's rays, shone brightly against the rich green grass. Happiness found me in a similar village to the one I had grown up in. Playful, laughing children were a welcome change from the castle. My skin had grown wrinkled from the passing of time.

Patti directed me to the last day of my life. I found myself walking up a stony hill to the cave where my dragon still resided. His beautiful golden eyes welcomed me. The smoothness of his greenish purple scales, beneath my touch, comforted us both. But I couldn't hold back the tears. For the first time, I wasn't ready to leave this plane. Through my sobs, I told Patti, "He is my best friend. We protected each other. People will not understand that he is gentle and kind. What will become of him after I'm gone?" I can still feel the sadness as I write this.

As I ascended, Patti suggested I look down. Maybe I could gain insight as to the geographical location. I saw a castle. There was a river running behind it. The land was clear surrounding the castle, with just a few tree lines nearby.

"A wise and loving being steps forward," said Patti's voice.

It was Merlin! His words, "My dear, you were to learn the ways of nature and magic." Then Mohra's parents come forward. My mother's hair was also fire red, my father's was salt-and-pepper. They wanted to tell me that everything had to happen as it had for a reason. It was necessary in order for me to learn from Merlin. "Release any guilt you have been carrying for not being there when we were attacked," they conveyed. Well, open the flood gates! I began to sob.

I heard Patti say, "It's safe to smell again."

I could feel the pulse of energy in my nose. *I must look like Rudolf the Red-Nosed Reindeer,* I thought.

Then an awareness of energy in the middle of my chest, the heart chakra, became present. Words from a previous regression came forward: "You can't have the light without the dark."

Once Patti helped me emerge from hypnosis, she mentioned that she had been tempted to take a picture of my nose. She noted that it had gotten quite red, more than just the normal would have been from someone crying. Boy, just when you think you're getting used to the countryside, a whole new land of dragons, Merlin, and magic shows up! Come on, Spirit, don't fail me now. Give me some validation of this last journey.

Upon waking the next morning, there was a feeling of freedom—but, more than that, lightness that had not been there before. There were also two dreams. In the first, I had dreamed of smelling mandarin orange very clearly. The second was of a footbridge. There was someone on the other side encouraging me to cross, as it was safe. My sinuses felt clear and open that morning. So I went around my studio, trying to smell the essential oils that I sold. All the while, I was repeating Patti's words, "It is safe to smell." I was met with some success and was hopeful.

Later that day, while giving a massage, I was aware of a

client's body odor, not in a negative way. Heck, *any* smell was good. This was a first for me, and it was so encouraging. That same day, per my request, Spirit showed up with an unusual validation. Again, it came while I was giving a massage. A client was telling me about a recent fall she had taken. She mentioned that she had hurt her nose and how she looked like Rudolf the Red-Nosed Reindeer!

The second validation showed up the next day. While scrolling the program guide on the TV, "The Disappearance of Maura" went by. I almost missed it, due to the different spelling—M-a-u-r-a, as opposed to M-o-h-r-a. But having had a best friend in grade school named Laura, I managed to catch it. Yes, Spirit, I was paying attention. Ok, but what about my dragon?

The next day, as I scrolled through Facebook, there it was. A dragon claw bench showed up. That satisfied me. Faith and trust were restored.

Over the next few weeks, my sense of smell would ebb and flow. No matter how many positive affirmations I said, I couldn't "will it" to improve beyond where it was. At least I had some smell, so I knew a shift was beginning to take place. And now, I had a real destination on my travel itinerary.

Another insight came, once again, about a week before I was to see Patti. The soul's "travel brochures" seemed to pop in when the mind was quiet. For me, that was when I was massaging. Waving tall grass in a sunlit meadow began to enter my awareness. A face—that of a young girl, maybe six—began to appear. Penetrating ice blue eyes, coupled with golden-white hair that surrounded an even paler skin, "glowed" in the sun's rays. The glow seemed to be emanating more from the inside. It was a love that flowed from her. Was this another past life as this young girl? Ah, I was a young boy *with* her. The love I felt with her and for her, pulled me in like a tractor beam. Mesmerized by her joyous smile and radiant face, I couldn't seem to look away. The names Sven and Gilda popped in. Was she my soulmate? Time may tell.

Chapter 8

A Two for One Trip

Up until this point, I had always traveled to one destination/lifetime. The exception was during the very first regression, where I remained in San Francisco but in different years. My journey now had an agenda—locate my sense of smell and activate it. But how many more "stops" would I make before the journey was over, the puzzle complete?

A week after my *vision* of Sven and Gilda, I was back in Patti's office, ready to explore again. My smell had continued its "ebb-and-flow" pattern. I was determined we would be successful in our mission, and so, going into hypnosis, we stated that intention. Well, lo and behold, there was a door to go through this time. It was a large wooden door, with what seemed to be metal attached. I got a sense it was old, and darkness surrounded it.

As I walked through, I found myself on a cobblestone street with small wooden structures around. Judging by the clothing of the many people I saw roaming about, I believed it was in the 1500s in England. I wasn't quite sure of the city—Berkshire, perhaps. I realized I was a man in my thirties. "When I snap my fingers, you'll tell me your name," Patti instructed.

"Samuel, Samuel Wilson."

As I glance around, I could see I was in a town square. It felt dirty and dark.

Continuing to survey my surroundings, I started to notice a tightness and a heaviness across my shoulders. My position in the recliner hadn't changed. We were entering new territory for me. I had felt chakras, things in my body afterward, but now, energy was showing up *during* a regression. It was giving me insights as to what was going on! This was another layer of energy, perhaps. As I relayed what I was seeing to Patti, the tightness and heavy sensation started to intensify, to a level that was starting to be uncomfortable. Soon, a mild panic started to creep in, as it felt almost like a weight on my shoulders was pushing me over. My mind kicked in. *This is really uncomfortable. We need to move on. I don't like this feeling."* I decided to share this with Patti.

"Reach up and see if you can feel anything," was her helpful guidance. In my mind, I reached around my shoulders. Oh my gosh, I was feeling wood. I was in the stockade! (I later learned, doing research, that it was known as a pillory.) As soon as that awareness hit me, the discomfort was gone.

"You are there, because?" Patti wondered.

Much to my surprise and regret, I had shot and killed my wife, Mary's, lover, Jacob.

A building in the square drew my attention. I saw a man in the doorway, wearing a bloodied white apron, a butcher perhaps. The odd thing was that I smelled formaldehyde when I looked over at him. Great, a smell. But how I knew it was formaldehyde, I didn't know.

Back to my crime. I was sent to prison for many years. There were several men to a cell. The whole scene was dark and depressing.

By the time I earned my freedom, I was an old man. Again, I had found employment in the horse stables. Unlike my lifetime as a slave, where I worked *with* the horses, this was a dirty job of cleaning up after them.

Well, I was ready to end that lonely, regret-filled life—which did end when I contracted pneumonia. My lesson from that lifetime, "There is power in the pause." How different things could've been if I had paused.

For the first time, Patti chose to lead me into another lifetime.

There it was, the lifetime I had "previewed" during that massage. I was beginning to think that, with this regression process, the layers of energy dissolved away, revealing deeper into the soul's journey. I had entered into the lifetime of Sven. My insight was correct. Gilda was there too. Only this time, there wasn't a sunlit meadow. On the contrary, it was dark, and young Gilda was crying as she reached out for me from a wagon. I sensed her family was moving away. It was hard for me to see her in pain, knowing there was nothing I could do to help. Would I ever see her again? I wondered.

Patti had me move time forward. I was a grown man in my thirties now. "Quite buff," I told Patti. I resided in the Alps with my wife, Marjorie, and our five children, four girls and a boy. The farming and tending of cows kept me in tip-top shape, hence the "buffness," I suppose.

"Move time forward to the next significant event," said Patti's voice.

My second to the youngest daughter, Danielle, had taken sick with a fever. I could see her frail body lying in a bed near a fire. Danielle died. This horrific event had taken place during the winter months. "We must wait for spring to bury her when the ground has thawed," I informed Patti.

We'd chosen a beautiful large tree that stood in solitude on a hillside to lay her to rest. I was standing alone at her graveside when I was hit by a realization. "Gilda! Danielle was my Gilda, reincarnated!" The shock of losing her twice was too much to bear. I suffered a heart attack and died on the spot. And for a fleeting moment during that event, there was a tightness in my chest as I lay reclined.

As I ascended, who was there to greet me, but Gilda! I was so excited. Patti instructed me to look into her eyes. "Does your soul recognize a connection?"

As I stared into Gilda's eyes, she evolved into my guardian angel. Now it made sense. The pureness of love and joy she conveyed from her *being* that day in the massage room was from an angelic realm! She wanted me to know, "All there is, is love."

She stood there holding an ancient book. The title on this rather large, heavy book that sported a tattered cloth cover was *Veil*.

"Open it. Does it say anything?" Patti guided.

There was a passage. "Your smell is just on the other side of the veil. It will come back to you."

It wasn't until the very end of the regression that the original shoulder discomfort I'd experienced from earlier as Samuel was totally gone. And by that point, I was pretty worn out.

Never being much of a history buff, I needed to do some research on Samuel's life in England. First, I looked up "prisons and stockades, 1500s." I discovered that what I'd thought was the stockade was really a pillory. The stockade was where your feet were placed in the device. I was learning something new, always a plus. I was surprised by the fact that, between 1350 and 1850 in England, it was basically a requirement that every town and village had pillories and stockades. And they were often displayed in the town squares! I also discovered that many prisons during that time housed multiple prisoners in one cell. But what really made my jaw drop was when I searched images under, "English prisons." There it was—the door, the original door I had walked through at the start of the regression! Holy cow, it was large, wooden, and grayish in color, resembling metal. I had to share this with Patti!

Where would my journey take me next? I couldn't wait to find out!

Chapter 9

Where There's Smoke, Is There Fire?

The road map had become a treasure map. And my sense of smell was the treasure. But what else might we discover before we reached our destination? December rolled around, and once again, a regression. By now, I was totally comfortable with the whole process. Trusting in Spirit and in my soul's wisdom, I found that any anxiety I'd had in the beginning was now gone.

As had happened before, I found myself without any doors to go through and really no cues either. So, I waited in the in-between place with my walking sticks of faith and trust. It didn't take long before I started getting a sense of very large green leaves around me. Clarity arrived! I relayed to Patti, "I'm in a jungle. I sense it's in South America somewhere." I'd become quite comfortable, having been through this process many times now, anticipating Patti's questions. I gave her as much information as I could.

My small male frame led me to believe I was around six years of age. My dark skin, along with my dark, coarse hair, said *native*. A smell of sweet flower flowed into my awareness. I believed this was what had caused me to wander off, and now I was lost.

Day turned into night. Strangely, there was a sense of peace as I heard the night jungle. But even at this age, there was a fearful respect, knowing I could be prey. As day broke, I heard a swiftly moving river nearby. I decided to follow it downstream. As I was lying in the recliner, I became aware of a pressure beginning to build over my eyes. The energy was showing up again in my present body, just like it had during the last regression. I relayed what I was experiencing to Patti. The "imprint" of energy began to magnify up to my brow bone and then around my head.

Oh my gosh, I was blindfolded! The top of my head started pulsing with energy. I continued sharing this with Patti, along with the realization, "I have been kidnapped!"

"Can you describe the kidnapper?" Patti inquired.

Even though I am blindfolded, I was aware the man who had me captive was a tall, very thin dark man, holding a long spear. Also, the smell of that sweet flower was present again.

"Move time forward," Patti guided.

Still blindfolded, I found myself in a tent/hut, my hands tied. *Boom, boom.* The energy pulsed at the top of my head. Smoke began to replace the fragrant smell of the flower. Guessing it was the campfire of those who had kidnapped me, I was then struck with a horrible thought. *I believe them to be cannibals!*

New Perspectives, Past Lives

No sooner had I relayed this to Patti, my throat was being slit. Instantaneously, I was floating above my six-year-old body as Moab. The pulsing in my head disappeared. A sense of sadness came over me. Teary-eyed, I told Patti, "I was only a little boy."

Patti suggested that, as I ascended, I look around to see if I knew geographically where I was. Hmmm, I saw brownish hills that bordered on mountain-like rose above a lush green jungle. I was still unsure.

"A wise and loving being comes to you now," Patti guided.

I was reminded of the Grizzly Adams character from my youth. This broad-shouldered "mountain man" with a jovial smile that radiated through a full beard was before me. Seeing his strong, rough hands oddly brought me comfort. He had messages for me: "Stop. Smell the flowers. But you need not go any farther than your own backyard."

I was told there was still another lifetime to explore—one that had been revealed to me, once again, while I was giving a massage.

While I was still in hypnosis, the life of Marybeth Williamson opened into my awareness. It was Colonial times in New England by the looks of the buildings as I walked the sunlit street through town. My tall, slender twenty-something frame was dressed very conservatively. My medium brown hair was neatly pulled back in a bun. I believed we were nearing the summer season, judging by the warmth of the sun on my face. My spirit was light and happy, as I was met with smiles from everyone who passed by. The sense was that I was well known and liked.

"Go to the place where you live," Patti's voice guided.

As I approached a large, wooden, two-story house, it lent me to believe that we were fairly well off financially—"we" being my husband, Robert, and our infant son, Steven. There was a sense that Robert worked in finances, either in the shipyard or for a shipping company.

As Patti snapped her fingers for a name where Robert worked, "Merrick" came to me.

Patti had me move time forward. It was now night, and I was at the shipyard. There was a structure fire, and I feared that Robert was trapped inside. As I relayed all this to Patti, an awareness of energetic clues began—this time, on the back of my neck and base of my skull. I felt pressure. Then the insight followed. I'd entered the burning structure, thinking I may find Robert. I realized a beam had fallen and hit me on the back of my neck, pinning me to the ground. I succumbed to smoke inhalation and passed away.

But unlike the last time, the sensation I was feeling didn't leave once the insight came. The pressure remained on my neck area. I was also aware of an emotional detachment as I rose above my body. It felt odd to me. It wasn't the norm.

The mountain man was waiting for me. The aching continued in my head and neck region. He had me face away from him. As he lightly brushed down my shoulders and arms, the sensation melted away. I relayed all of this to Patti. As that sensation, energy, released, so did the tears. With their cascade, my throat area began to get this feeling of coolness. The coolness expanded from my jawline down to the top of my chest. It radiated outward like the mist on a mountaintop. There was this sense of clearing layers of energy that were in the throat chakra, built up over many lifetimes, perhaps.

The mountain man told me, "If you visualize the brushing effect I did on your shoulders, you will be able to move the energy yourself." He then had me turn around to face him. When he took my hands, which seemed so small in his, there was such a peaceful, lighthearted, happy feeling conveyed that any lingering sadness was quickly replaced with gratitude for the wonderful life I'd had as Marybeth.

Patti had begun to emerge me from hypnosis, when a realization hit me. My mountain man was Father Time!

As with every session, afterward, Patti and I discussed what had gone on and any insights that we may have. We'd noticed, especially in the sessions regarding the intention to smell, a common thread was smoke. Marybeth died from smoke inhalation. Moab, the six year-old in the jungle, smelled the campfire smoke just before his throat was slit. Then there was Mohra, who smelled her village burning in Scotland. I also wondered about the fact that my mother smoked while pregnant with me and still does to this day. Could that be a factor to connecting past and present? Another question arose: Could my life as Marybeth be a contributing factor to the anxiety I felt today when in a situation where I feel I can't breathe?

The journey was far from over. Little did I know where it would lead and the treasures that would be discovered along the way.

Chapter 10

The Staycation

Traveling, seeing new places, and having new adventures is exciting. But sometimes it's nice to stick closer to home. I was really starting to see progress in my quest to regain my sense of smell. But the time in between my last regression and the next was wrought with worry and stress over a health issue my dad was facing.

It was agreed that we would enter into February 2018's regression with the intention "whatever is for my highest good." I had no idea I was about to visit a lifetime/place that was familiar to me.

So, during these months of working with Patti, I'd found myself in an interesting situation, as if enough shifts weren't already taking place! Throughout my life, I'd had premonitions in dreams, high intuition, and even a couple out-of-body experiences. But now, something new got my attention and caught me totally off guard.

During those times in between the regressions, as I stated earlier, my guy and I would go bass fishing. One of our favorite lakes to fish was Lake Kissimmee. Sitting in that beautiful lake is a magnificent 3,300-acre island, known as Braham Island. Its eleven and a half miles of shoreline have some wonderful fishing spots. On a good day, we are gifted with the sight of deer, buffalo, and bald eagles that all reside there. Beyond my love of nature, I'd never given much thought to it, until one particular Sunday. As we were fishing around the island, as we had multiple times before, we entered into a small cove on the south side. This energetic surge of peace moved through my soul. It was so powerful that I made him stop the boat. *What is this connectedness I'm feeling?* I wondered. It was an experience unlike any other I'd ever had. I had to sit on the back of the boat and stare at the shoreline. Somehow, I had to capture this moment and tuck it away into a deeper part of myself. Where was this *pull* coming from? Had the regression work shifted an energy? Peeled a layer? I wanted to bathe in it all day. But after about ten to fifteen minutes, my guy was ready to move on and fish.

With each visit to Lake Kissimmee, usually twice a month, I insisted we visit that shoreline. I was curious to see if the feeling remained. Not only did it remain, but it also intensified to this "tractor beam" of sorts. It was all I could do not to swim to the shoreline. There was a need, yes *need*, to walk this land. There were two things stopping me—alligators and a twenty-four-hour surveillance system on the island. It is privately owned. My mind heard, "Spirit resides here." What was this all about? I was close to finding out.

So, come February, as I sank into Patti's recliner, her words guided me into hypnosis, and the answers began to unfold. Tall, golden grasses, gently pushed by the wind, came into view. I walked as Red Wolf on the land known as Brahma Island today. My brother, Seven Eagles, accompanied me. My buckskin hung gently off my twenty-year-old hips. Our beautiful, long, black hair hung loose. We were good together. Joy and playfulness were in the air. I was "schooling" my sixteen-year-old brother in the art of hunting.

"Move time forward. Where do you live?" Patti inquired.

Our village, with many teepees, resided on the mainland. I was aware my family also consisted of two younger sisters and another younger brother.

Patti directed, "You'll tell me what year it is." She snapped her fingers.

"It's 1703," was my reply.

Again, I began to receive energetic cues in my body. I notice a lightheadedness, bordering on dizziness, starting in my head. I'd learned to wait for the insight to follow. I let Patti know what I was feeling. The insight unfolded. I, Red Wolf, was lying on the ground.

"Rewind the tape just before that happened," Patti instructed.

My horse had been spooked by a snake and had thrown me off. I'd hit my head on a rock and broken my neck! I was alive but paralyzed. Then the realization came. I wouldn't be alive for long. Sadness was released down my cheeks with the knowledge that I would not be able to teach Seven Eagles the *way*.

My vision was now of Brahma Island. The stars in the vast expansiveness brought peace to my soul—much as they did in my Hopi life and still do to this day. I'd been taken to the island by the elders of the tribe to make my final journey. They chanted prayers throughout the night. I died.

Finally, the dizziness was subsiding, only to be replaced by a feeling of confinement. Aha, my body was being prepared. They'd wrapped me in cloth, and my body was placed on a platform about six feet off the ground. I shared this all with Patti. Then, while lying on the platform, I was shown the elders around a fire, chanting, the belief being that smoke would carry their prayers to the Great Spirit.

Just as this was being revealed to me, Patti went into a coughing fit—the kind where water was needed to stop it. "Is there smoke?" she inquired through her coughs.

"Why, yes," I told her, as I had not conveyed that detail to her yet.

As I ascended, I was greeted by Seven Eagles. He reminded me, "I am you, and you are me. We will be together again."

"What is the lesson you were supposed to learn?" Patti asked.

"Interconnectedness," I replied.

"A wise and loving being comes forward," Patti guided.

It was Sitting Bull.

Patti instructed me to follow him to a room with many crystals. She told me to lie down. "A brilliant light shines through the crystals, targeting where you need to heal," she suggested.

I revealed that it was my heart. This next part was so auditory it was almost as if Sitting Bull was speaking through me. "Don't be afraid to love. Letting go is part of it, but we are all one."

Patti wondered, "Is there any other places the crystals shine?"

Oddly enough, my feet! "Ground yourself with Mother Earth. She is wise!" Again, I heard Sitting Bull's voice so clearly. It felt like him, instead of me, conveying the message to Patti.

With that, Patti guided me out of the regression.

A few days later, a *lightning bolt* hit me. The crystals on my feet, the desire and undeniable pull to *walk* on Brahma Island. *Bam!* The last time I'd been there, I'd been paralyzed and unable to. Finally, after months of wondering what the connection was, it all made sense. A piece of the puzzle was put into place.

Spirit also had a message that was delivered in an unexpected, unique, and subtle way—perhaps to see if I was listening. Shortly after my session, as I was driving to work one morning. I found myself behind a slow driver. Generally, I don't have much patience for this sort of thing, and I usually pass slow drivers. This morning, instead of doing that, a thought entered my head. *They'll turn soon.* So, I followed. *Finally,* the driver did turn, right into the drive I was going to, Starbucks.

Yes, they're parking. I was headed through the drive-through; peace restored. *No.* As I went around the corner after receiving my order, guess who was backing out?! Frustration filled my words as I asked Spirit "What is it I need to know?"

The license plate of the car once again in front of me was "0-3-7." Wait a minute; those numbers were in the year of Red Wolf, 1703. Maybe it was less about the year and more about the actual numbers. So, I consulted my go-to for numbers, *Sacred Scribe Angel Numbers*. The number *307* spoke of your life's purpose and of encouragement from angels and ascended masters. It also spoke of skills and talents to be a spiritual teacher and/or healer to assist others on their spiritual awakening. That was feeling pretty accurate at the moment. And the number *307* related to the angel number *1*, the sum of all three numbers when added together. It was about thinking positive and letting go of fears. There they were, all four numbers in Red Wolf's year. Once again, Spirit confirmed I was on the right path. As I listened to the radio a couple days later, the DJs remarked about Mardi Gras. The first one was held in 1703!

So, our next regression was scheduled to be videotaped. Patti wanted people to see what this "work" was all about, as did I. Little did we know, it would be one of the most profound journeys yet for me and crucial for retrieving my sense of smell!

Chapter 11

The Light at the End of the Tunnel

Sometimes, the people we meet when traveling can be a breath of fresh air, others are a pain in the rump or a fleeting romance, and still others turn out to be lifelong friends. And if you travel with a companion long enough, you soon gain a greater understanding of that person. So what if those trips spanned many lifetimes?

This next regression was slightly different. First, it was being videotaped, which meant no music for the relaxation part and overhead lighting (usually there are just lamps). Though a little distracted, I still managed to go into hypnosis with ease. Our course was plotted—find my sense of smell. I soon had an awareness of fog. Then the scene began to unfold. There was a large sailing vessel; this grand wooden structure was my home.

I was an old deckhand named Matt. The work was hard, but I was content.

"Rewind the tape. What led you to be here?" Patti wondered.

"My mother died giving birth. Eventually, my father didn't know what to do to care for me. So, as a young boy, he asked if the captain of a ship would take me." I had always fancied ships and the sea. I was not upset.

The ship I now resided on was the *Meriweather*, I believed. Our home port was England.

"What is the ship's purpose?" Patti inquired.

We hauled cargo for trade, often visiting the Caribbean, specifically Barbados for fruit, cloth, and so on. Then I started getting this sense that we were lost at sea. This struck me as being strange. We were experienced sailors, and our captain was very good. Then it started unfolding that the crew had been infected with some sort of plague. Often, ships that had been infected were not allowed to dock, I would later learn. Eventually, I too fell ill with coughing and fever, and then came death.

I didn't find this lifetime overly emotional for me. Apparently, I was saving that for the next one! In Matt's life, the lesson was to learn teamwork. After I ascended, my mother from that life greeted me. There was so much love and tenderness.

Patti, in her infinite wisdom and intuition, sensed there was another lifetime to be looked at related to my lack of smelling. She instructed me to go back into another life that had everything to do with why I was there today. "Let it unfold," I heard her voice say.

It was the Caribbean again. This time, I was a four-year-old

New Perspectives, Past Lives

native girl, Sebina. My mother and I were picking fruit. We were very close.

Patti had me move time forward. There was a palm tree on a beach. I was now in my twenties, standing in front of the tree.

"What happens next?" Patti inquired.

Well, this was a first. The scene went dark. I relayed this to Patti, also telling her, "It's as if I've been snuffed out."

Patti then suggests I rewind the tape back ten minutes before that happened. A man was choking me. Oh my gosh, he was my husband! He choked me to death! Tears began to flow down my cheeks.

Patti had me ascend, and for the first time, I realized the "lesson I was supposed to learn" was unclear. My wonderful Father Time, aka the mountain man, was there to greet me. He was a very safe, comforting male figure for me. My Caribbean husband was now standing before me, asking for forgiveness. Patti suggested I see him as a young boy. "What do you see?"

He was loving, sweet, and happy; my heart opened. Then she had me view him around the age of twelve. He grew sad and angry because of an abusive father. Sadness overflowed in me. This beautiful soul was lost and hurting. Hate and anger were created from pain.

Patti had me look into his eyes. "Does your soul recognize a connection?"

As I looked, there was something, like an object far out on the horizon, but I couldn't quite pinpoint it. I was then brought back to the "here and now."

Like many times after the session, I got up and went to use

the restroom. While I was in there, it came like a tsunami of realization and knowledge crashing down on me, so overtaking me with emotion that any attempt to hold back the tears would have been futile. My Caribbean husband and the man I was currently involved with were one and the same! Instantaneously, answers to questions I wasn't even aware I was asking flooded in. There was this intense knowing that we were soul mates, brought back together to heal that past lifetime. Explanations of intense reactions to situations that never made sense before came to light. With tears streaming down my face, I reentered the room with Patti and Bobbie, the videographer, and shared the discoveries I'd made just moments ago.

It was as if I had opened a tomb of lost artifacts, each one filling a piece of a large puzzle. I shared with Patti and Bobbie the intense fear I felt with my present guy during his anger-filled outbursts when he was under the influence of alcohol, how literally gut-wrenching it was. I also shared how I knew that confrontation at that time would only make things worse. I had no reference for this behavior from my current life. Then there was why I had fought so hard to hold on to "us," when letting go would have been easier. I had seen glimpses into his heart and knew there was good there, even when he had doubts. And I recalled the instant connection and energy in our first kisses that literally took my words away. My soul *knew* all of that. With Patti and my work, I now *re*-remembered.

Wow, even today, as I write this over a year later, the layers still peel, and the tears still come—not tears of pain but of amazement, peace, and freedom. And as I drove home that day,

New Perspectives, Past Lives

the word *freed* kept coming to mind. I felt like I finally had the full picture. But did I?

My travels were beginning to feel lighter. Some interesting things happened later that day. Out of all the regressions Patti and I had done, well over half a dozen, this was the first time my guy asked, "Was I in any of them?"

This is a man, who unlike me, claims to be very concrete in thinking, not believing in spirits, and certainly not past lives. We never talked about my sessions, other than the fact that my sense of smell was coming back. And yet, somewhere, deep inside, I believe his soul knew and somehow felt a *shift*. As we lay next to each other in bed that night, my hand on his bare chest, I got this strong smell of coconut. So I inquired if he had used sunscreen that day, knowing full well he hadn't. The man never does. But I had to ask anyway.

His reply was what I had expected. "No."

Now wait a minute. If I related the smell of coconut to sunscreen, then at some point, I had to have been able to smell. And yet, prior to meeting Patti, I never remembered having had or having lost my sense of smell.

My ability to smell was really coming along. And although I couldn't necessarily identify the smells themselves, I was consciously smelling *every day*! Little did I know what "artifact" was coming next.

Chapter 12

An Unexpected Trip

Shortly after my last regression, I was heading up to Michigan. My father had taken a turn for the worse following his open-heart surgery. Two strokes and two weeks after the surgery, he was left fairly incapacitated. In the cold of winter, there I was, putting on layers—sweaters, coat, and gloves. But there were those unseen layers too, smiles and support for both Mom and Dad hiding my concern.

Dad spent most of his time sleeping, barely opening his eyes even when he became alert to eat. Communication was tough, but his acknowledgement of my presence, him saying my name, and his mannerisms assured me that *he* was still "in there." I had never shared with my parents any of the regression work I was doing with Patti. I had been raised Lutheran, and they still were devout in their faith. We'd had reincarnation discussions in the past, and I knew that at least my mother did not share in my belief. Right about the time I'd felt like I wanted to share what I had been doing, the diagnosis for congestive heart failure had come for my dad. So, I'd remained quiet. Looking back, I realize now that divine timing was at work.

That first night after my arrival, my mother and I left the hospital. Spirit brought me the perfect opportunity to share what I had been doing. My mother was in her kitchen, and I was in the dining room when I smelled the nastiest thing I had smelled since my sense of smelling had started to come back—her cigarette. She has always been a smoker, even during her three pregnancies. I entered the kitchen and said, "You know, I can smell that," pointing at her cigarette.

She quickly apologized, not quite grasping what I was trying to convey.

"No. I can *smell* that. Want to know how?"

With a stunned look, she replied, "Yes."

I proceeded to share with her about my work with Patti, without going into too much detail, for it was late, and we were both tired. Surprisingly, she was receptive, dare I say, even curious. Well, that was a relief, for all along, I had anticipated a lecture. Funny, we never quite stop being in that parent-child relationship, no matter what the age. What came as an even bigger surprise was what she told me next. As I was explaining about the regressions, she remarked," I remember when you fell out of the tree and lost your sense of smell."

Wait, what?! Now remember, I had never remembered

having a sense of smell *or* losing it. I did, however, remember the tree incident.

Around the age of eleven, I had climbed a familiar tree in our backyard. It wasn't the first time I had done that. Well, for whatever reason, on that summer day, as I grabbed ahold of a low branch and swung out, I let go. Falling about four feet, I landed smack on my tailbone, my back hitting the ground and knocking the wind out of me. I came down so hard, in fact, that I recall gripping at the grass and telling myself, *just breathe*. I was unable to walk. A friend carried me into the house. Everything turned out to be okay, except, apparently, my sense of smell.

As if her statement didn't shock me enough, what I found just as amazing was the fact that she remembered nothing else about the incident, except the smell part. And that was the one thing I didn't remember. She held the *random key*, unlocking that piece of baggage for me.

Talk about divine timing! Had I revealed to my folks about the regressions in the fall, when I had planned, I would not have experienced the lifetime as Sebina yet. Was there a connection to her being choked to death and my not being able to breathe after the fall? The energies seemed the same. And did Spirit bring Mom's cigarette smell to me purposefully so we would have that conversation? My guy smokes and I had never smelled his cigarettes. And what *was* the connection between not breathing and smell? Still so many questions remained unanswered.

When we pull back the layers, shifting the energy, releasing blockages, creating a ripple effect, and revealing answers to mysteries, the effects can be far-reaching. And what a gift I was given, with the circumstances being what they were. Ah, yes, the circumstances—sitting in that hospital room, knowing he was still in there, only waking to eat. It left me wondering, *Where do you go, Dad, when you sleep?*

Chapter 13

The Ultimate Journey

*L*eaving a loved one and knowing it will be the last "goodbye" is very hard. Dad and I shared a piece of lemon meringue pie for my birthday, and then I headed back to Florida. He was heading to Hospice, unfortunately.

Around this time, my nephew and his wife were expecting their first child, a boy. With my dad's time of transition drawing closer, so too was the due date of the baby. My mother claimed that my dad was waiting for him to be born, before he would make his final journey and "let go."

I also believe during this time that Dad paid me a visit. One night, during my sleep, he came to me in a dream. This had happened before with other people and animals, *after* they had passed on. In the dream, I went to answer a knock at the door. My dad stepped in, not the current eighty-five-year-old version, but as a young man in his late twenties or early thirties. His age didn't surprise me. What did was the fact that he was at my home and not the hospital.

"What are you doing? You're supposed to be at the hospital," was all I could remark before waking.

I appreciated the visit that night, but this was just the beginning of a multitude of amazing moments.

Right around Sunday of that last week that my dad would be with us, I began receiving the message, "Thursday" and "timing," over and over in my head. I believed Thursday was to be his departure date but wasn't sure what timing meant. Tuesday, I had an appointment with Patti scheduled. With Dad in Hospice and time ticking down, I was quite emotional. I still went. I knew the one place I should be was in that blue recliner, covered by that comfy quilt.

"This time," I inquired, "instead of going into a past life, could I try and locate where my dad may be?" I had long held the belief most people in the stage of life he was in travel back and forth between worlds and that he was now doing so.

So that became our focus. The induction into hypnosis and moving forward felt longer than it had in the past sessions. As Patti guided me to "go even higher," I could literally feel an ascension of sorts. When I had reached that higher realm, Patti inquired, "What do you see?"

"There are individual lights as far as the eye can see. They are all souls."

Even as I write this, I am in awe and gratitude to have been able to see into this side.

"See if you can locate your father," Patti encouraged. I found him, only not in a physical form. He, himself, was light. "He is being cradled by many smaller lights. I think they're angels." I relayed this to Patti. "He's in a place of rest. I'm unable to communicate with him," I explained.

"Notice if anyone comes forward," Patti responded.

Keep in mind, all who came forward are deceased. First was my Aunt C., Dad's oldest sister. She was leading the way, as she had in life. Next was my Aunt H., his youngest sister. Her smile radiated from ear to ear. There was such excitement to see him. There was a feeling of anticipation, much like waiting to see a loved one walk off a plane. Her presence was strong. For a brief moment, his mother, Helen, was there. But then, his father, Herbert, was present. This caught me by surprise. He had passed a long time ago, when I was a teen. He and I were never close. I was being told that he would be there to help my dad cross. He'd been waiting a long time.

"Are there any questions you would like to ask?" I heard Patti's voice ask.

"Yes. Is there any connection between my dad and my nephew's soon-to-be-born son?"

I heard the answer in my mind. *That is not of your concern at this time.* And then, *Remember.*

I was now being shown a lush, green oasis of sorts. There was a beautiful waterfall as a focal point. Many people of all ages, races, and time periods were about. I understood this to be a place of renewal. Time didn't exist in this realm, just an immense sense of love, peace, and acceptance. Before I left, I thanked the ascended masters and guides for allowing me to see and remember this realm. A message came before I went. I heard, *It's all timing, divine timing.*

Patti guided me out of hypnosis. I felt a sense of happiness for my dad. And yet, the grief remaining for us was very present. By the next day, Wednesday, a text brought the news that my nephew's wife was in labor. I was continuing to get the message "Thursday" and "timing." Was Thursday to be Dad's departure day?

Wednesday afternoon at 1:40, I began a massage on one of my regular clients. Her clothes were draped on a chair off to the side of the massage table. Her rubber-soled shoes were there too. Only one was on the floor, and the other was atop a two-inch-wide leg coming from the base of a heat lamp. At two o'clock, we heard this *thud.* It was loud enough that my client remarked, "What was that?"

In disbelief, I responded, "That would be your shoe. It flipped off the stand." Upside down, I might add!

I was nowhere near the stand at the time. And the reason I knew it was two o'clock was because I immediately checked the time. You see, a dear friend once said, "Death is like kicking off a tight shoe." I had never forgotten that and wondered, Was that Dad's departure? I thought, for sure, when I checked my phone after her session, there would be a missed call—the one I had been anticipating and dreading. It was not there.

When I left work that evening, the very first word that came out of the radio was *timing*! Whoa, Spirit! Later that Wednesday evening, after I arrived home, I received a text letting me know that my nephew's son had come into this world at 3:11 that afternoon. At 12:30, Thursday morning, my phone rang. Well, I knew before answering, this was the call I had been dreading all week. Mom's voice came over the line. "Hospice just called. Dad passed."

My session with Patti, the shoe, hearing "Thursday" and "timing"—it all left me wondering. I believe that Dad's soul transitioned that Wednesday afternoon, and the shoe was my sign. But if so, that left questions. Ah yes, me and those "questions." Can the body survive without the soul for short periods of time? Was there a connection with the baby? Did Dad wait for his arrival? *Or* did he come back *as* my nephew's son? Is that what I saw in my session with Patti, when I saw dad being "cradled" by angels?

It was very possible those questions might never get answered. But I trusted, if Spirit thought I should know, then surely, I would get the communication I need. I would *remember*, as I was told from the other side. *My* journey was not over, not by a long shot!

Chapter 14

Journey Back to the Islands

Upon returning from Michigan, after my father's funeral, it was time to see Patti again. Although my sense of smell was beginning to return, Patti and I both agreed the full treasure had not been uncovered yet. Again, this regression was being videotaped. The lighting was a little different this time; no overheads were on. This made it more comfortable.

Once I was relaxed, Patti had me imagine the fall from the tree and the feeling it had given me. "What is the next thing you see?" she inquired.

I was Sebina again, in the Caribbean. It was nighttime. A large fire was ablaze on the beach. My husband, Stromer, and I were arguing. I started to become aware of a sensation at about the level of my collar bones. I relayed this to Patti. I was angry that the ongoing problem of him "stepping out" on me was still, well, ongoing. My anger and hurt took over, and I began to hit him. Now there was an awareness of an *ache* just off center and over my right brow as I lay there. What was this all about?

My husband was trying to stop my abuse, and we ended up hitting our heads against one another. The mystery was revealed. Things escalated and got out of hand. He began choking me. Blinded by emotion, he was unaware of what he was doing until it was too late. I slowly fell, limp, to the sand, dead. As I began to ascend, a headache started on the back, left side of my head. I relayed this to Patti.

"Pull it out. Tell me, what is the size and color of it?"

I was holding a large, black mass in the palm of my hand.

"What does it represent?" Patti inquired.

I realized it was guilt, anger, and hurt. As this became apparent, the mass liquefied through my fingers, gone. First, of all, I felt angry and hurt that he didn't love me the way I needed him to. But also, I felt guilt for putting all the blame on him. After seeing through a small window of Sebina's life in the first regression, I felt victimized. But now, I realized, having seen a broader vision, that I was responsible too. That was Sebina's life lesson—take personal responsibility for your life and the choices you make in it.

I needed to see him, my husband. I needed to ask his forgiveness for blaming him this whole time. And I needed to forgive myself. Patti had me imagine him in front of me. Patti suggested I repeat the words, "I forgive you for not loving me the way I needed you to. I forgive you and set you free. By setting you free, I set myself free."

I repeat those words out loud. They helped; my headache was gone. A supreme being stepped forward. At first, it was Father Time who showed up, my Grizzly Adams figure. But he quickly changed to my dad! Immediately, tears flowed down my cheeks. He had words. "Even on this side, I love and support you." Boy, that was a surprise and emotionally intense.

Patti guided me out of hypnosis.

I began looking through the layers, to make sense of it all. The rational part of my conscious mind was trying to convince me that this lifetime in the Caribbean was just me trying to work out my current relationship. But my soul knew better. The angels had been sending me messages weeks before my guy and I had found each other. They kept showing me double numbers—*33, 22, 77*, and so on—throughout my daily activities. I recognized the signal but didn't understand the meaning. It became clear once I met my man. As I wrote his name on a piece of paper for the first time, it hit me. His first and last name had three letters that repeated themselves, in the same order, in both names! The angels were letting me know to be on the lookout for him. I believed this was a second chance for us to get it right and heal the Caribbean lifetime. My guy and I were both student and teacher for each other.

Sebina's life lesson of taking personal responsibility was something I had continued to work on in this lifetime. I had been learning better boundaries and *my* responsibility to enforce them. I still was sifting through the guilt that arose at times in doing so. The guilt itself was somewhat of a mystery. And occasionally, that sensation in the back, left side of my head—the place where I kept the anger, hurt, and guilt—still revealed that my work wasn't quite finished yet. I had learned that the energies move and shift in their own divine time. I had made boundless discoveries, and yet something was still missing.

Chapter 15

The Final Piece

My sense of smell was apparent every day now. It seemed, as time went on, it only improved. But I couldn't help but feel that one piece of the "treasure map puzzle" was still missing. There was a *knowing* that Patti's and my work together was not quite finished.

Going into hypnosis was a piece of cake now. This time, however, we took a different "route" than we usually do. Once I was in hypnosis, Patti had me stand in front of large, ancient, wooden doors. "A wise being meets you there. Who do you see?" Patti suggested.

He was a tall, hooded, robed figure with no face, known as the Ancient One. Upon entering the building, he guided me down a row in between two very tall bookshelves. A book, its cover grass green, caught my eye. The edges of the pages were gold so, when the book was closed, a brilliant gold shimmer, surrounded the three sides. What happened next was odd.

"Take it. Does it have a title?" Patti wondered.

There was neither title nor words inside; everything was completely blank—as if it were still unwritten. The future perhaps?

Then I started to get a sense of water. Here it came. I was a younger male, floating in a boat or raft, I think. The tan uniform of a pilot was on my body. England was who I fought for.

"Rewind the tape to before you were floating," Patti suggested.

My copilot and I were returning from a mission. We were over the Indian Ocean.

"What is your name?" asked Patti's voice.

"Captain Mark Whitaker," seemed to leave my mouth. I wasn't sure of the year—1902, 1920? It was unclear. I became aware of a right engine failure. We'd ended up crashing in the ocean. I was the only survivor. Oh, now I realized, there was no boat. I was in a life jacket. Soon, a smell of some type of mechanical fluid came into my awareness.

As I relayed this to Patti, a sensation began in my abdomen. It was an energetic clue alerting me to the fact that, as Mark, I had suffered an internal injury. At first, after crashing, I felt very lonely. But as my passing drew near, this peace came over me, and a smell of vanilla replaced the mechanical fuel smell. I then noticed the warmth of the sun and the beauty in the way it reflected off the water, as if I was seeing it for the first time.

New Perspectives, Past Lives

Perhaps I was delirious from my injuries. After passing, I was met by my copilot on the other side. He reassured me, "It's all good."

Aha! The book had a title, *Peace*.

Patti spoke to the Ancient One. "Is there another lifetime Shari needs to see?"

I was led down another aisle. There was a large, dark, *very* heavy book, which I retrieved. As I held it, my sense of smell started leading the way. Sweet cake—it *was* cake, a birthday cake for me.

Now, you may want to buckle in; this is going to get bumpy. The image started to come in— brown hair in ringlets; a little girl around five; time period, 1700s to 1800s. This was me. As I looked around, the scene looked like the 1960s. The people, clothing, and architecture all resembled the '60s. "This doesn't make sense," I told Patti. It felt as if I was viewing one of my lives, only from another lifetime's eyes. It was as if I was watching a movie and playing the lead role. Patti assured me that I should just go with it.

Okay. I felt myself being drawn to the pool. There was this sense that I had drowned in it. "Rise above and look down at yourself. What do you see?" she suggested.

I was a younger woman with short blond hair, facedown.

"But this doesn't make sense," I insisted. I felt like I was in one life, viewing one of my other ones.

Patti continued to reassure me that it was okay. Then a realization hit me. "I have committed suicide! I took a bunch of pills and just walked into the pool," I told Patti, shocked.

"Because?" she inquired.

My eight-year-old son was killed by a car while riding his bike. I couldn't cope with the loss.

Why was I viewing it this way? I just kept saying, "This doesn't make sense." What *was* coming through loud and clear were details. My name was Nancy Koehler; I was living in San Diego, California. And as if all of this wasn't odd enough, I found it strange that I was more upset at the fact that I had committed suicide than I was about losing my son.

Once on the other side, I was reunited with my son. It felt good to hug him again. But I was aware that there was a different feeling upon passing this time than there had been during the past regressions. I got a sense that suicides were handled differently. I heard the term "fractured soul." The Ancient One sat me down, stood behind me, and placed his hands on my shoulders. I was told he was "reintegrating" me "into whole." After this, I was pure light.

See, now aren't you glad you "buckled in?".

Once Patti brought me out of the regression, I was left feeling tired and just as confused as I was during the regression. Patti didn't have any answers either. "You mean the student stumped the teacher?!"

We laughed.

The questions flowed through my mind. Had I viewed Nancy from another life because the emotions were too painful? Or was it because I was so medicated that I wasn't aware enough as Nancy? And why was I more upset about taking my own life than I was about losing my son? Would Spirit validate any of this?

A few days later, Spirit did just that. While I was watching TV, there were three references made about San Diego, California, on three separate shows.

But what about everything else? Would any of it ever make sense?

Chapter 16

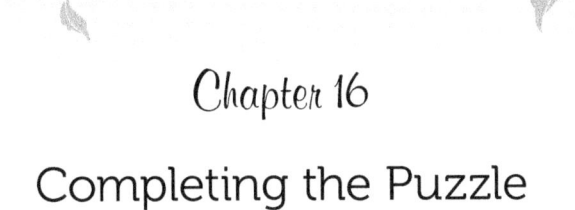

Completing the Puzzle

You know when you're packing to head home from your journey and making a place for everything in your suitcase, not only your original belongings, but also the ones you accumulated along the way—trying to make it all fit. Patti and I still had unfinished business. We both wanted to understand my last regression. And we weren't quite "packed up" yet.

As I was going into hypnosis, eyes closed, I began seeing the color purple. This was familiar to me. I often saw this when I was getting a massage. To me, it was a signal that the energy was moving. Patti was taking me to higher realms to connect with my guides. My focus seemed to be fixated on my eyes and the purple. Then, like an elevator reaching its destination, the purple disappeared. Patti suggested that a guide, someone to help me, come forward. I saw an angel come into view. Without words, I was told his name was Michael. His wavy, light brown, shoulder-length hair reached his white robe. There was a knowing that he was there for protection.

About this time, that familiar "cake" (vanilla) smell from the last regression was apparent. The energy was building in my head, and I began to cry. The coolness in my throat area started, like it had done before in a previous regression. Only this time, there was a tightening, a restriction, that accompanied it. The pressure continued to build near the base of my throat. I realized that this was about my past life in the Caribbean and the choking. Residual energy seemed to be fueling my tears. Angel Michael had me lay my head in the palms of his hands, which were full of light now. There was a sense that, *I've got you. It's safe.*

My attention seemed to be shifting to my feet. They were physically crossed at the ankles, as I lay in the recliner. There was a darkness and a stillness associated with the feeling. I wanted to move them, but I felt unable to. I was getting the sense that they were bound together. My attention then started to be drawn to a tree beside me. It had a large trunk and was big, perhaps an oak. Oh, I was strung up by my feet, hanging from the tree. It was me, Samuel, from my slave life, being whipped. Still feeling the feet, I felt clarity shine through. As I was being whipped, my thought was, *Go inside. Take it. Survive!*

Oh my gosh, another moment of clarity arrived. The thought of Nancy's suicide took me by surprise because giving up was and *is* not in my nature!

I began to sob. As I let the grief flow—the grief that, as

Nancy, I had *numbed* out—Angel Michael was there as protector to provide a safe place for this. His hands were now placed on me, one cradled under the back of my head and the other covering my forehead. I got a sense that he placed the one on my forehead over the third-eye chakra to help me *see*. As my sobs continued, the focus with my feet began to subside. Then my dad showed up to offer love and support—which, of course, refueled the tears.

Finally, all the pieces of the "smell puzzle" felt like they were completed and in place. The suicide life was so painful that I could only view it through another lifetime's eyes. The Samuel, slave life, connected to the fact that I was sadder that I had given up, taking my life as Nancy, than I was over my son's death. And Archangel Michael gave me the protection I needed to allow the grief, which I had blocked in a few lifetimes, to really flow and release. Certain lifetimes, woven together like a basket, held my sense of smell. There was purpose in *everything*! There was always divine timing at work. I felt cleared and safe to truly smell again. Grief was nothing to fear. It was just a part of loving. And yet, there was still one question left to be answered.

Chapter 17

Coming Home

No matter how exciting, fun, and adventuresome the journey, it always feels good to come home. There you find the grounding of routine, seeing loved ones with a new appreciation and they for you, the security in the familiar. And with those "adventures" we bring back "souvenirs"—perhaps new friendships, knowledge and appreciation of foreign lands and cultures, maybe a stronger sense of self—trinkets to remind us of it all. But before I could walk through that "last door" of home, one more question needed an answer: What was the common thread holding the basket together? What was that emotion that linked all those lifetimes of smell together.

Let's see, the first lifetime that started the shift of my smell was Mohra in Scotland. The smell of smoke took me into the regression. The feelings of guilt and helplessness were present when I was unable to save my village. Then there was Moab, the six-year-old in the jungle. I smelled the smoke from the campfire just before my throat was slit. The feeling was of being helpless. Next was the big one, Sebina in the Caribbean. The smoke from the campfire was present when I was being choked to death. There was both guilt and helplessness associated with that life. And then there was, Nancy, who was unable to save her son. Could there be any greater sense of helplessness than not being able to save your own child? And did falling out of the tree in my youth trigger that "response" with my smell because of the inability to walk for a brief time and not being able to breath? Smoke was prevalent in so many of the regressions, and the smell of my mom's cigarette smoke that night prompted the information that located such an important piece of the puzzle—the piece that connected my present life to a past one.

They were all part of that "basket" holding my sense of smell. It wasn't until I was emailing Patti regarding the emotional connection that I had the *aha* moment that I had been seeking. As soon as I was typing about Mohra and how "I felt so helpless that I couldn't do anything," there it was! It shone as a golden thread woven in the basket—helplessness! We found it, Patti and I together! Our journey had lasted over two years. The journey had started out of curiosity and had grown into this mission to locate where my sense of smell was hiding, just waiting to be discovered.

But little did I realize that, during this *quest for treasure*, my sense of smell, I had been peeling back the layers of energy—self-doubt, fear of acceptance, misunderstood gifts—all those layers we all have that dull our light, preventing us from shining brightly. I discovered that the treasure was the journey itself. And I discovered that *coming home* was loving and recognizing my true and authentic soul—a destination/treasure I had been seeking for most of my life. This is a place that, when fully embraced, is secure and grounding no matter life's circumstances. There, self-love and acceptance are as strong as any brick or steel wall. Once I'd found it, there was no going back. By subtracting the layers, I had, indeed, added pieces—the pieces that made me feel whole. The layers were gone, and I was free.

Thank you to all, who have traveled with me, allowing me to be your guide. May *all* our lights shine brightly, pushing back the darkness and illuminating a path.

Acknowledgments

To my always supportive man, Tracy, who may not understand or even agree with these concepts but still believes in me. I'm so glad we found each other again.

To a special client and friend, Marcella Zinner, who started me down this path of curiosity. Thank you for *seeing* me.

To Connie Lowe, a good friend and client who assisted me with the technical side of this project. Your guidance and input were greatly appreciated.

To all my other clients, who listened with open hearts as I excitedly shared each regression, your support was strengthening.

A special thanks to Patricia McGivern. You started this journey as a guide and became a beloved friend. Your open mind and beautiful soul allowed me to heal in so many unexpected ways. For that, I am eternally grateful.

About the Author

Shari A. Hinkle has worked in the healing arts as a licensed massage therapist since fall 1994.

Her work as a therapeutic touch practitioner, along with her sensitivities to energy, offers a unique view to past-life regression work.

Her experiences with Patricia McGivern were so profound she became a certified hypnotist through Omni Hypnosis Training International so that she may bring healing to people on a deep level.

Since 2000, Shari has been using her gifts to help her clients heal—mind, body, and soul—through her business, New Perspectives Body Care.

You may contact the author through her website: Newperspectivesmassage.com

CPSIA information can be obtained
at www.ICGtesting.com
Printed in the USA
FSHW011625240919
62341FS

9 781982 233457